73

First edition.
ISBN: 978-1938912856

Cover Design by Derrick C. Brown
Interior Layout by Winona León
Edited by Jessica Abughattas and Derrick C. Brown
Proofread by Keaton Maddox
Author Photo by Kurt Heyde

Type set in Bergamo from www.theleagueofmoveabletype.com

Printed in the USA

Write Bloody Publishing
Los Angeles, CA

Support Independent Presses
writebloody.com

A Constellation of Half-Lives

ᚼ

poems by Seema Reza

Write Bloody Publishing

Los Angeles, CA

writebloody.com

Dear Reader,

I am an American mother. For nearly two decades, my government has been sending my neighbors and their children to war in my name, against people who look like me.

There, but for the grace of God, go I.

This project began as a series of second-person poems exploring the uneven distribution of grace and became a cycle of poems addressing an imagined (though not quite fictional) woman named Khadija, a mother living directly in the path of the destruction and environmental contamination of the Global War on Terror. There are letters to other American civilians, to my sons, to veterans, to my sisters and mother, to people I have hurt and to people who have hurt me. There are many letters written to the reflection of myself I find whenever I look closely at *other*.

It is my finger on the trigger, me kneeling beside the burial mound, my body nestled in the wooden box. There is no grace. There are only points of light scattered across a blackening sky.

I have tried to capture both the expanding darkness and the glow of a precarious, ordinary life in these pages. I hope you catch a glimmer of your own reflection while reading them.

Yours,

Seema Reza

For my mother, her mother, & her mother
For us: the children we were
& them: the children who did not survive

A Constellation of Half-Lives

A Constellation of Half-Lives

∴

∴

The horrors that we have seen, the still greater horrors we shall presently see, are not signs that rebels, insubordinate, untamable men are increasing in number throughout the world, but rather that there is a constant increase in the number of obedient, docile men.

—George Bernanos

Dear Khadija

Somewhere beneath this pink moon you

mourn a child

into the soft terrain of your cupped palms
you whisper the verses
we were taught as children

Inna lillahi wa inna ilayhi raji'un

∴

When was the last time your mother pulled a comb through
  your hair, divided the black strands into
        three sections & crossed them tightly?

  Have you forgiven her betrayal?

∴

What is common between a helmet
    & hands cupped over the hollows of eyes
        how does a flak jacket relate to a veil to
        red lips high heels the drag
              of razor over knee cap?

∴

What is it to exist within the confines of your skin
    what aches have you stopped noticing
        what grief causes your limp
              whose voice speaks to you
                  from the mirror?

∴

humanity obscured by layers
of Kevlar & camouflage,
you would not recognize him in a line-up

if mothers like you were allowed such a thing

he fears sleep, sees your son in dim hallways &
shiny shopping malls, in museums
built to honor men like him

Reconciliation

I.

Long ago I was a leaf turning my face to the sun. The muscled shoulders of the lioness were mine. I waited for a breeze. The hair on my body protected me. My soft belly was my wealth.

II.

bending to lace shoes with calloused thumbs
humming in a broken voice along a dangerous path
     adding water to stretch the soup
     raising torches in the street
     teaching a father to read
     building a wall
     weeping with a neighbor

devotion & destruction in
every scarred moment

III.

We sent you into harm's way. We put you into situations where atrocities were possible. We share responsibility with you: for all that you have seen, for all that you have done, for all that you have failed to do.[1]

---

1 In reconciliation ceremonies for veterans, Unitarian Universalist Minister Chris Antal leads civilians to recite this phrase.

IV.

a force of heat-seeking miracles

complete &
fragment
shatter &
rebound
slinking ribs
pulsing organs
the unyielding grace of shin bone
crease & purple bloom
keen & failing senses
hunger & thirst
desire
scattering like shrapnel
hunted by foxes / like foxes

FORTUNE

I am not supposed to know what it means to *pass someone the AK* I
am not supposed to know that sometimes people get killed because they
[we] all look alike & retaliation does not always require   accuracy
I am an American civilian I am absolutely not supposed to
know how often a child **holding a gun** or a child holding a cell
phone or a child holding a long string attached to a paper kite rocking
in the sky is shot & killed in my name I am not supposed to know
that there's no way out of this that four thousand more troops is
the integer some undetermined number is the exponent & the
figure represents nightmares per night on Earth I'm not supposed to
know that the Afghan boy he shot on his last deployment the one
that brought him spinning into my life looked just like my son but
smaller & less lucky & his mother who is less lucky than me must
know all these things too

[Dear Khadija] Unspecial Women

Yet, under the realities of organized male territoriality and aggression, when women produce sons, they are literally working for the army.
—Adrienne Rich
Of Woman Born: Motherhood as Experience and Institution

I.

Decades ago our bodies were swollen maps
& we pressed fingers to
flesh pulled taut over
our sons' turning bodies,
heavy & throbbing for light & release

How foolishly we pushed them forth screaming,
kept them alive despite their impulses
toward self-destruction

As though this time it would be different
& our sons would not suffer like our fathers
or their own

II.

Khadija, did you love your son's father?
Did you lift at the sight of his lined face?
Trace his scars with your lips
reach for his hard hand as you fell asleep?

Or do decades of panic humming
between skin & bones strip desire
of the expectation of joy?

Is worry over loving your body
absurd when around you bodies flicker?
Intersections of miracle & curse
Weak sources of cruelty & pleasure

Delicate bags of blood threatening to spill

III.

there must have been ordinary days:
hot sun on clean wet hair
bright things jingling at your wrists

the happy regret of eating too much
& laying with full belly under the ceiling fan
days when nothing *happened*

& you held your children's hands & crossed
the road without fear
daydreamed while picking vegetables
returned with loaves to an unshattered home

IV.

I am soft, bending, addicted to comfort
I've done nothing to deserve

I'm a kind woman, pretty, unspecial
cruel, impatient, unforgiving
entitled & swaggering & American

faced with violence
I am certain
I would surrender immediately

 except: on ordinary days
 when the children kick one another
 under the table & the air conditioner & oven
 are running at once

I cannot convince myself
that you were not here yesterday
that I could not be there tomorrow

Reckoning with Impermanence
for Ali

Why is the measure of love loss?

—Jeanette Winterson
Written on the Body

I. I try to impress upon memory

his black curls,
slack cheeks & shining lips
his live, deep,
even, breathing

it is not expertise or hard work but luck, exhaustible,
which has kept him safe from kidnapping,
dry-drowning, catching a rare disease,
drinking poison, choking on plastic,
chasing an errant ball into
the path of a drunk or careless driver

I whisper *forgive me*
His eyes blink open

The beauty is so oppressive, I ache

II. Every answer a surrender

Beauty is so oppressive, we ache

His wish: to see from both windows at once
Mine: to live dumb as a cow by the sea

We park on a ledge & watch waves grow & fizzle
He wonders at dark spots on the water's surface
& I point to the low clouds
whose perfect shadows slide dark
across shimmering water & mountainside
Ah. He knows & won't ask again

We share the loaded backpack, lose our way
Eat peanut butter & beef jerky
Lay on boulders in the rain then return to the car

We travel in silence, not who we were

III. You can't really love anything until it's over
(antemeridian)

we travel in silence, point as we go

the summer after I turned ten
my father & I walked
waist/thigh deep in clear water
stepped on sea urchins
& kept walking

I didn't know it couldn't last:

a father's warm hand
a too big swimsuit &
sweet fish for dinner

the summer after I turned ten my father & I
walked waist/thigh deep in clear water

archipelago of bodies in a chain

IV. I am a fraud & he is a fool

Archipelago of bodies
My hair graying, his smooth cheeks erupting
into roughness. The road winds then straightens.
Dusty & wild, we re-enter the grid

(I first brought him here sixteen years ago
a milk-fat comma on my hip, overjoyed
by the revelation of my face from behind blanket or hands)

I promise: *I will always be right here*
He learns object permanence
Yes. I tell him. Or else *No.* He nods, accepts.
He trusts I can take care of us both

None of these things are true
I need him to believe so I can too

V. Mistakes in the shape of a person

I need him to believe so I can too
I put him on a plane & drive away
Stop at the ocean's edge
Stand with my hands on my own shoulders

Further south, a man honks
from the next lane then follows
as I turn at the park
drive past my destination
until he gives up or tires of the sport

Ma, you were right
        without a father in the driver's seat
        without a husband or diamond ring

I am nothing but a pile of neatly folded promises

VI. I dream terrible things

I am nothing but a pile of neatly folded promises
a regular woman,
taxpaying nurturer

> I am afraid of coming unzipped/
> I long to unleash my teeth

unencumbered, without the tension
of gratitude & repulsion for my body

I don't often tell stories about him but
sometimes I shine light on a glimmer
& stir the undercurrent of regret

A sediment of rage rests beneath,
which, disturbed, weights
the floating feather of anecdote

VII. Suspended in a cliff over a waterfall

floating feather of anecdote:

One year I sped up the East coast
Threaded the red car along
the walls of mountains
spent two nights in a yellow cottage

had dinner & pie with a man
I couldn't know until
he stopped vying for my impossible love
& loved someone else

I took the ferry-way home
Drove onboard & faced the wind

There's no position more powerful
than being the one gliding away, waving

VIII. Never mind. This poem isn't about that

The gliding shadow of joy
Temporarily dimming
the steady sun of loss

He's been leaving since his first breath
rendered the placenta   the first thing I made for him   useless

I watch four ducklings nestle & rearrange
on the bank of the pond
Their mother shifts her weight between webbed feet

She cannot count, but she understands the odds

Just half a year ago, before motherhood weighted her
she paddled the feathered bag of her body
on the water's surface thinking only of fish

All of this is ordinary

IX. It is bitter cold

An ordinary Thursday in February
Snow is falling & a father
in borrowed scrubs
a surgical mask
tented across his mouth & nose

receives a wailing baby with circles under her eyes

He peers at her through thick lenses & is pleased

Though he deserved a son

she almost arrived
     in the car in the wheelchair in the elevator

In such a rush to trade the familiar dark of her mother
for a bright cold place
She may never grow to love

X. If joy is conjoined with loss

I must love this quivering world
the infant lolling into milk-drunk sleep
confident in her mother's palm
the father polishing his shoes
confident in the morning
the gasping lovers parting
confident in one another's intention

the steadfast certainty
that the worst thing has not yet happened

I'd surrender possibility
For the assurance of no new losses
but all I'm promised is growing distance
from the wreckage of my mother's childhood

XI. When he's outgrown me, he will remember

wreckage of his childhood:

    wailing in a house of pointed fingers
    my hands on the wheel of a car
    sliding out of control.
    Unswept floor & power
    disconnected. The steep stairwell
    unlit hallway sticky floors
    broken dishes
    crying baby.
    The unyielding sharpness
    of the father. The growing
    discontent of

the flawed mother in the rush of morning

XII. *this was our new table once*

the flawed mother in the wine-red silence
walking through mossy halls of memory
trying to remember:

    the prized rubber ball, leather baseball glove
    preferred dishes, playing cards, binoculars
    rocking chair, fraying favorite blanket
    laughter, trash talk
    someone enraged
    someone scolded for gloating
while around us everything
quietly corrodes
polymer chains unfastening
molecules floating free in the air

XII.a (I am too old to be enraged at my parents)

the flawed mother in widowed silence
her impenetrable denial,
her passive lamentation *Anyway, what to do*
her unquestionable, imperfect affection

the hot-tempered father, his tepid remorse
he taught us to accept apologies without
expecting change, to approximate the distance
between thunderclap & lightning strike
the crude practice of clearing our hurt with laughter

they did not protect me from my reckless
stupidity, or from their weakness & tempers

the wood paneled basement, heavy furniture & brocade

it has all faded, has all been disassembled

XIII. Lonely & relieved

We have all been disassembled & freed
Disillusioned by our mothers
Seeing clearly the smallness of our fathers
whose hands were once immense

My sons' raging responsible father
Their selfish, ill-prepared mother

May we be more
mothered than our mothers
More fathered than our fathers

We haven't got a choice
except to turn away

I am shrinking in the rearview

What's done is done

XIV. I must forgive you

Anyway, what to do. What's done is done.
Haven't you forgiven me?

We are each less
than the other needed
More than anyone deserved

Slithering through our lives
without footholds

Forgiveness means only
that it is neither
my responsibility
nor my right

to punish you for my pain

for who I have become

Sam

For a year, you lived as an extension of me
    your needs & mine intertwined

There were days when you would not sleep
    could not cease crying at the ordinary traumas

    of becoming human:

        sharp teeth tearing through
        the flesh of your pink wet mouth
        bones lengthening, calcifying,
        stepping toward rigidity

When did your knees become so hard? Your elbows?

It happened in bits, while we slept

Young lives are like fire, they can be used to burn a city down or illuminate the darkness.

—Jimmy Santiago Baca
The Lucia Poems

[Dear Khadija] Military-Aged Males

Yesterday I stood in his bedroom & examined him:

>   uncalloused hands, stubbled cheeks,
>   thick curls, unlined brow

then pulled back the covers & shook him from dreams

He's become a military-aged male
has registered & if selected
& given a gun to point

>   He'll shoot, because he hasn't got a choice

ALLAHU AKBAR

I didn't teach him the tender threes of ablution,
palms cupping water & dragging
again   again   &   again
lowering clean forehead to earth under the high dome

I never taught him to remove his shoes &
raise stiff hands alongside his face, turn side-to-side
shoulder-to-shoulder with boys like him
thumbing flimsy holy pages

He'll learn on the job to beg for mercy
on a classroom floor in this town or in
the smoke of a gunfight on distant soil

I raised him without faith in a god
who could save us
and does not want to

[Dear Khadija] American Violence

Has news of the killings reached you yet?

Last week soldiers barricaded the mouths
of city streets with tanks while our children
lifted signs & screamed for their lives

We lined behind, gape-mouthed, helpless
then trudged peacefully home to pay bills
wash our cars & eat sweet fatty things
on soft chairs facing our televisions

Outside the clouds stretched west toward us.

This year not one of the schoolyard children
remembers when the war began or why

More sons & daughters have been carried limp
from our schools than their mothers & fathers
have been draped in a striped flag & shipped flat
from armed tours of your dusty city streets

Do you shrug or smile at this, Khadija?

∴

The first instruction of active shooter lockdown
fire drills are outdated
is turn off the lights, make yourself disappear
dial your mother, whisper goodbye

When the gunman opens the door
to fire into the cowering silence,
pop-up surprise party style, create chaos
Lift & launch heavy books
Hail Mary
the news will name you martyr

                    The mother of a martyr is martyr herself
                    Do you shrug or smile at this, Khadija?

HELP

Tell me what you know about dismemberment.

—Bhanu Kapil
The Vertical Interrogation of Strangers

I know the sharp curve of the boti[1]
its iron feet held down by calloused flesh
on the concrete floor of a hot kitchen

I know how it feels to have a heart cleaved
to have feet in more places than I have legs
To feel torn & made whole
by the same sharp thing
my tongue keeps thirsting for

my children cut from me
their hungry mouths & hands
reaching as they recede

I know what it is to let someone
cut my voice from my throat
& leave my smile intact

---

1 A boti is a long, curved blade that cuts on a platform held down by the foot.

[Dear Khadija] The torpid inertia of *Insha'Allah*

∴

We are not young
    less beautiful than we were
        (more beautiful than we'll be next year)

Our daughters are consumed
    & our sons are gunpowder & uranium
        packed & loaded

Hate Academy

The inter-subjective is something that exists within the communication network linking the subjective consciousness of many individuals. If a single individual changes his or her beliefs, or even dies, it is of little importance. However, if most individuals in the network die or change their beliefs, the inter-subjective phenomenon will mutate or disappear.

—Yuval Noah Harari
Sapiens

You know things I did not teach you, teach me things
I don't know: about the Knights of Camelot & Abraham Lincoln,
tectonic plates & the remote control.

Read this, you say. *Read this.* You hand me a book
I haven't read, open to a passage about the British
Hate Academy, an idea born to prevent
Shell Shock   Soldier's Heart   PTSD
desensitizing young men by showing them
—teaching them to crave kill
before they know the cost.

You read over my shoulder,
shake your head, waiting. Certain this is yet another thing
I simply do not know.

I close the book, inhale, unsurprised. *They still do this.*
I hide my fingers in your hair, you put your head on my shoulder.
    Tears form in the corners of your eyes. I watch
an innocence I had forgotten   leave you.

I press my lips to your forehead. *It doesn't work.*
Not for any length of time. That's why it hurts when they come home.
I whisper a promise I cannot keep,
We will end wars with love.

You look up at me. Half-smile, kiss my cheek.
Mistake this far reach
for an innocence of my own. Again, the burden
of telling me what you know & I don't is upon you.

It won't work, Mama. There's too many of them.

EXCLUSIONS

You know, every day, many important papers come across my desk in that marvelous Oval Office, and very few items remain there for long. Got to keep that paper moving or you get inundated. Your snorkel will fill up and there will be no justice.

—George H.W. Bush, September 1991

An envelope marked *important*
contains my new insurance policy
I scan the pages and catch the word war
under the heading *exclusions*
I am unconcerned

War does not come to Maryland

War hatches across the river in solemn buildings
filled with suits & flies
across the ocean to nest
in the land of my children's ancestors

Bundled beneath the blankets
under the humming blades of the ceiling fan
my son leans his head against my shoulder

I balance a cup of coffee, the first
of the day's quiet luxuries
the sky lightens & we listen to the radio

a missile whistles to landing
a bazaar breaks out in gun fire
a car explodes taking down a wall

his long eyelashes
cast shadows on ruddy cheeks still
sticky from yesterday's dessert

QUARTERING

No Soldier shall, in time of peace be quartered in any house, without the consent of the Owner, nor in time of war, but in a manner to be prescribed by law.
　　　—The Third Amendment of the United States Constitution

When the soldier knocks on your door,
billet book in hand, move aside
to let him enter.

He will wipe his feet, remove his hat
　　(you'll learn to call it a cover).
He will be polite, place his rifle by the door.

Treat him with reverence, keep your fear
hidden from view. When the question
of whether he's killed bubbles up in your throat,
thank him instead　　　　for his service.
Say you *can't imagine the sacrifice.*

When little streams of sand pour out of his pockets
& form mountains on your floor, be gracious—
　　look away while he sweeps the grains
　　back into the creases they emerged from.

Make small talk with the soldier you are quartering,
invite him to eat with the family, make space for him
in front of the television, catch him up on celebrity gossip
he missed at war.

Offer to make up the couch, though it is likely he will decline
& unroll his sleeping bag; he's grown unused to comfort.
He will have identified weaknesses
　　in your floor plan
　　& adjusted for them

Insist on providing a pillow　　　　to ease your conscience

If you come out for a glass of water in the middle of the night,
see the orange pill bottles lined up on the granite counter.
He may tell you what they're for or you can guess
when your children complain at breakfast
about their sleep interrupted by his night terrors.
    Shush them.

Order a noise machine to obstruct his screams.
    Tell them *this is only temporary*.

When he steps out to smoke a cigarette in the dark try not to see
the glowing deposits of depleted uranium beneath his skin
    turning his body into a constellation of half-lives.

Soon you will call a warning before you switch on
the garbage disposal & coffee grinder.
Apologize when the door slams.
Reassure him when the neighbor's car backfires.
Never leave the door unlocked.

He will begin to tell you stories in which violence is the setting,
not the point, a piece of the landscape of the places he has visited.
Then he'll tell you what he knows about death.
    Do not flinch.
    If he cries, nod.

You notice yourself worrying when America bobs in place
watching the world, ready to pounce like a double-dutch champion.
    The word *troops* means something different
    when you're quartering a soldier.

You may notice him making plans, initiating conversation,
sitting down more often to beat the kids
at video games.
His laughter less a cough, his anger more a flash
of lightning than a storm.

You will wish to share his burden, sleep without the sound barrier,
hear his cries in the night.
For all his straight-backed composure
        he is no machine.

Lie awake & wonder if this is worth the tax incentives.

You're in too deep now, but remember your words—
this is only temporary—
orders will arrive & his bag—never fully unpacked—
will be shut tight, his boots laced, his dusty rifle cleaned.

Feel the tension in his parting embrace
the recoil as he adjusts his cover
& looks away from your tears
Realize your every act of kindness has been an act of war.

Tomahawk

Tonight, I call on all civilized nations to join us in seeking to end the slaughter and bloodshed in Syria, and also to end terrorism of all kinds and all types.
—Donald J. Trump, April 6, 2017

The fire alarm sounds in the hallway.
I am on the ninth floor
in the purple tank top I wore yesterday
shuffling stacks of mail.

I am head of household & according to the IRS
have paid more than my share to repair
the lightly pocked highways I drive & send columns of fire
into crumbling cities I've never seen.
There will be a refund.

The alarm is still sounding beyond
my bedroom, past my sons' empty beds,
the blank television & the chained
door of my apartment. I consider my jeans
hanging behind the bathroom door, think of
fastening a bra around my ribcage, pulling something warm
over my shoulders & assembling on the sidewalk
with my neighbors, their cats in boxes
& bundled children.

Instead I shut the bedroom door,
plug the crack with a rug, muffle the wails
& keep tearing promises & demands & admonitions
into jagged pieces & wait.
The alarm continues.
Surely this will come to an end.

April 7, 2017

DRONES

you wonder what it would be like to touch a cloud

somewhere your brother

                          knows

how the sky tears open

    with a whistle & scream

        until clouds touch earth

"IF BABA GETS REMARRIED, IT'S REALLY OVER BETWEEN THE TWO OF YOU."

My son
cups the
glowing
wick
of a candle
already
blown
out &
calls it

light.

We are all trying to change what we fear into something beautiful.

—Kelli Russell Agodon
"Hunger"

Joy

does not want to be
written. It does not need me.
It is the orange light of knowing
each pretty moment is only
almost. Once, a man grabbed my arm
in a gesture of love & I shook for an hour
in the aftershock.

I CAN'T SLEEP

Last night the yellow teacup cracked clean in half while I washed it

& when I went out on the balcony to smoke a cigarette

the handle of the sliding door came off into my palm. My phone screen

is cracked & my favorite rings won't stay round.

In the bedroom you lay prone, parted lips twitching into an almost-smile

your eyes rocking gently beneath their lids, long arms reaching

toward my emptied space. It isn't that I don't love you just

things fall apart in my well-meaning hands.

AMMA, WHAT DO WOMEN WANT?

stiff doc martens billowing silk salwar kamiz
hemp bracelets brown eyes rimmed covergirl black
soft-cheeks vixen lips cleavage cleft and long necks
at the muslim community center our mothers

watch—envious, ashamed
our bodies like theirs & alien
they block our periphery with headscarves
teach us to move shoulder to shoulder:

bending at the waist hands flying
to thighs crossing the heart
index finger stabbing the devil
spines curled over femur bones
forehead to prayer hall carpet
face right then left greet angels
in unison

led by the hungry men
whose desires we must somehow
learn to manage from behind

BELEMNITE (*I DREAM YOU ARE IN MY BED*)

Disoriented by your smell
I can't remember your name
I dip my finger into the depression where
neck & shoulder & clavicle intersect
& ask, *Is it you? Are we here again?*

Never have the borders of my body been so blurred:
your flesh mine, my flesh yours.
The free exchange of fluids, the reckless drawing of blood:
There is no intimacy like a wrecking love.

Some nights I lay in (our) bed awake. These nights stretch.
I stand from the bed, sit on the toilet. Bore of masturbating.
Open & close books. Remove layers of blankets, layers of clothing.
Stand under the shower. Eat ripe fruit over the sink.
Wipe my face with a dishtowel.

These are my most honest nights.

Since the untangling the lovers have been kind & clumsy & graceful.
Hungry & apathetic. I couldn't say how many—it doesn't matter.
They are not enough.

Lately I prefer to find myself curled upright in the bathtub,
chin between the twin flats of my knees. When I am alone,
I am almost enough.

In daylight I face others propped upright, wounds dressed,
 wrapped in hard plaster. Underneath the casing I am all hollow.
        I think: *You are boring, boring, boring.*

I read many interesting things. I am so smart,
I read things most people wouldn't. While I read,
my mind wanders to fixate on men who think I'm great,
but not good enough. There are plenty of men like that
& they confirm what I recite in my head (in his voice):
        not enough, not enough, not enough.

When I meet a man like that, the longing is unbearable.

The last time you were in this bed, it stood in the little house we bought.
We had given up, you were on edge, drinking too much,
pacing late into the night. I'd pack for my impending move,
go to work & come home to find my things unpacked.

It was like that for us:
You showed love through bared teeth. I offered sex as sedative.
That last night you woke me. Stood over me with a flashlight asking,
Are you okay? You were crying out in your sleep.

I lifted the covers, allowed you to lay beside me.
To fuck dangerous men to sleep is not unlike the circus trick
of putting one's head into a lion's gaping mouth. There's a certain
glamour & giddiness to escaping unscathed.

But I never cry out in my sleep.

When dreaming of my own death, I fall silent.

CONSTRUCTION

There is nothing ordinary on our horizon
& we are here, busying our wet mouths

> *you pull my hair*
> *bite my neck*
> *my palms on your skull*

polite conversation, measured sips, averted gaze.
Beyond the glass window
dark against the red sky
the latticed necks of cranes
dangle empty hooks
from thick cables.

Operators home, loving their wives.

THIS POEM IS WANT—

1.

nights spent displacing
unnamed hungers from this bowl

ecstasy, clenching at my own hands
or the strange hands of a lover
only unearths more

2.

We spend the day arranging ourselves to avoid contact
but you linger on my mouth
my eyes touch
exposed clavicle under your loosened shirt

A wound reopens

3.

low hanging branch

leaves framing bright C of the moon

sweet wine in a jar

lips on my shoulder

PERMISSION
after David Allen Sullivan

Protect others from the mist that settles over you in the night.
Bury the quiver in your voice,
do not bow though you were taught to.

Write the poem about your fears:
your mother's breath stilling, your sons' faces
blue—or bearded—the imminence
of today disappearing into memory

Then write a poem about the fact
that you've never been faithful to anyone,
always kept one hand feeling along the walls
for a knob, a hinge, a latch
to release the pressure in the chamber

Let favorite songs be addressed to new lovers,
play the same notes & hope
for different endings

Be the only one to laugh at your jokes
have an apple & a sleeping pill
for dinner on Wednesday
view the sun through a kaleidoscope while your inbox fills

Say no to people you like, take what you want
do things your mother's way (though you swore you never would) or
allow the laundry to pile up & serve a breakfast of leftover dessert
smile at babies without yearning to press their plump cheeks to yours

You can cry about one thing when you are sad about another,
allow a man who won't solve your loneliness to hold you
his thick fingers cradling your skull, his smell entangled in your hair
even after you break free

SOLITUDE

The smell of scotch wafts from a mug
wedged between stacked books &

I'm up to my ears in blankets but there
isn't enough between my goose-fleshed thighs.

I listen to the apartment quietly alive
with its usual noises: maps taped to the wall

rustling in ceiling-fan wind, a passing train,
refrigerator hum, a faint beeping, a sawing sound

I cannot trace to a source. I can't tell if some of these
sounds are inside my head, & no one is here to tell me.

Suspended between

the dread of tomorrow & relief over the end of today,
my memories unvalidated, here I am alone & most alive,

a version of myself I almost love, though I do
nothing productive. Chuckle & berate myself & sometimes

awakened by the chattering of my own judgment
I rise from bed & dance softly in the almost-dark

city glow of my bedroom & with consideration at low volume
I play whatever song echoes inside & mouth the lyrics

shaking my arms & head, tiptoe the beat on the thick rug.
When the last notes sound I play the same song again.

1995

You can tell an American child by their shoes.
Americans keep their shoes dirty, but a child
just trying to look *American will keep her sneakers pristine.*

My mother is full of observations of white Americans
& brown ones like me, American to spite their parents.

Sometimes she thinks they (we) have no loyalty,
or generosity, or couth.
Other times she says *they are clean, but still,*
I am not to share their pants or sit on their toilets. She warns:
They wear their shoes all over the house,
their dining tables are cluttered with papers because they don't eat food.
Americans, my mother tells me, *don't care about their mothers.*
Whatever they might say, they think less of us.

She warns me & I don't believe her.
When yet another American boy discards my heart in favor of one
who I'm sure does not have hair on her knuckles

she says, *I don't know why you're so hopeful and soft-hearted.*
It's not my fault.

A LETTER TO MY COFFIN

She starved & gorged,
licked salt & color from
her fingers, pressed cold
bottles to her neck,
massaged calloused feet
with soft hands wiped
sweat from between
her breasts bit her own
tongue this limb bears the
memory of being kissed
from wrist to elbow
crease on a dark escalator
sliding underground.
This body held knives &
babies, soft balls of dough,
the rough faces of men.
Ran fingers through
beards, dragged teeth
against skin squeezed
with her thighs & released
them unharmed. She
rocked herself to sleep &
shuddered awake in the
dark. Hold her.

She earned this sturdy bed. This freedom from dreams.

THIRD PERSON

In the spreading space between you & I

a third person

who rose from the crash of our laughter & glowed
like a reflection caught in a dark window

                  is turning to mist.

This is no ordinary break up   it is a death.

I cannot fold it neatly, tie its ends
like a handkerchief
into the lines of stories I produce.

    This is a trick gone awry:

          a person is being sawed in half

WE ARE PREPARED

with hard-faced dolls whose plastic eyes shutter when laid flat // with combs & pink-tipped bottles that empty when tilted & no explanation of how a baby arrives in the body // what we must give to receive // what it takes to release it // We are prepared with toy guns & bruised cheeks // Told we must stand in the rain, lift heavier & heavier things // usher others toward doors we hold open // We have no choice but to stand & fight // our worth tied to our ability to perform harm // measured by fist crash // how we use our knowledge to make things explode // We arrive each morning teeth & hair brushed // soft creased faces cups of coffee to go // business casual trousers & dishonest statuses // We do our jobs, make small talk, smile back or smile first // long for love/ for rescue/ for relief/ for a good parking spot // We measure time by how much we have left to do // eat a pastry because we deserve it/feel worthless for breaking rules we set for ourselves // We go to yoga or the gym or happy hour // go home & eat dinner alone or with people we love // or should love or used to love or people // We wish would love us as we deserve to be loved // cry & laugh facing the television // wish we were different more beautiful/ more powerful/ better dressed then // brush our teeth again (the best among us floss) // We dip our fingers into pots of lotion & massage our own cheeks our ringed necks in an act of cherishing that is nearly obscene // mouths slack & stretched // We are tired, we keep coming up short

36

A lifetime isn't long enough for the beauty of this world
and the responsibilities of your life.

—Mary Oliver
The Leaf and The Cloud

Madness. Suicide. Murder.
Is there no way out but these?

—Adrienne Rich
"The Phenomenology of Anger"

1.

I've reached the age at which my grandmother
left seven wailing children to grow old & plump
in the absence of her shadow

Every day, the quickening pulse of my urge to dissolve.
I haven't got the guts, so odds are tomorrow will
knock on my eyelids demanding I open up
& answer the phone, the emails, tear envelopes
crush coffee beans

2.

None of it matters.

Not the books I've read or pretended to read,
not the vanished labor of dinners & laundry
& lust returned or refused or the ungrateful
row of orchids whose withering stalks I water faithfully
though they refuse to bloom.

3.

What will happen to my beautiful things,
my daring ideas, my ordinary
hungers? My heavy pots & precious
metals? Who will tidy the messes I've left,
the cluttered exuberance of my dumb human life?
Who will clear the debris of my desire,
my jagged plans for vengeance?

Not you
with your own stacks
& sweaters & socks, your filing
cabinets of tax returns, your collected
legacy of love & gracelessness
as important as mine which is to say:

not important at all.

4.

                                        open-armed leap,
                                        cyanide,
                                        gun to temple,
                                        weighted pocket slide
                                        into river or lake
                                        or pond or bathtub
                                        lungs filled with gas,
                                        fistful of pills,
                                        needle to the arm,
                                        laying on train tracks
                                        running barefoot into traffic

(I haven't got the guts)

5.

when I lived in the dark
row house in the suburbs
I woke each morning &
brought the yeast to life
under the correct conditions
    warm water, a spoon of sugar
allowed it to breathe & expand covered
then punched it.
Placed its heavy body
in a shallow metal pan
let it rise again, chastened.
Turned it solid
in the tomb of the oven.

Whether or not the yeast behaved as expected, we ate
& were full until we were hungry again
then started new yeast & consumed that too

Tell me: how am I different from this?
Tell me. Are you?

6.

You joined & divided in the dark
arrived glistening, gasping, thirsty & dumb,
keen to survive. Closed your gums
around the dark point of my milk-plump breast.
I allowed you. I should have blocked your airways with my palm
& spared you the burning drowning wild & concrete places
the cracking & sinking earth
the looming glass landscapes.
I offer you umbrage, a warm coat,
ice cream. Cherries & the pleasure of spitting pits
I show you the angled legs of crickets,
tadpoles swarming in the shallow, the blue heron stalking fish,
the dwindling whales through binocular sights

knowing you are the best thing here
    (until you are consumed)
I prop you at this table & am glad for your company.

Afterword:
Notes on Waking the Sleeping

I work things out in my dreams. My brain seems better able in the absence of my effort to guide it. A few years ago, I had a vivid nightmare that a child-sized demon was trying to force her way into my bedroom. I pushed on the inside of the door, and she pushed from the outside.

In the midst of this effort, I realized I did not have strength enough to keep her out nor did I have any weapon with which to overcome her. The thought occurred to me very clearly: *the only weapon I have is kindness.*

I opened the door and faced her. She was more terrifying than I could have imagined—horror movie scary, with blackened eyes and bloodied mouth. I took a breath and steadied myself, forced myself to look directly at her.

I asked, *Are you hungry?*

She nodded, and I led her through my dark apartment, trying to act as though she were an ordinary houseguest. I switched on the light above the dining table and gestured to a chair. She sat and I poured her a glass of milk. In the fruit basket were two bananas. One brown, spotted and half broken open, the other ripe, closed, yellow. I hesitated and thought: *She's just a demon child. She wouldn't know the difference, I could give her the broken banana.* But I reminded myself: *this is all you've got.*

I gave her the good banana and as she ate it and drank the milk, she turned into a regular little girl, scared and small and not at all threatening. Still in need of kindness. Though her humanity was obscured—by my fear or her hunger—though my kindness was borne from my own desire to survive, she was there, waiting for me to recognize myself in her.

What damage could I have done if I had acted out my fear as violence?

In *The Poet in the World*, Denise Levertov writes, *A struggle uninformed by love and compassion makes of the rebel a mirror image of the executioner.*

Our greatest obstacles in the work of repairing a broken world are not those who seek to defeat us—they have acknowledged our capacity, and in doing so have fortified us. Our greatest obstacles are those who are apathetic—those who insist upon keeping the bedclothes up over their faces, breathing only air that is warm, air they have breathed before.

In a 2014 interview with Krista Tippett, Buddhist scholar and environmental activist Dr. Joanna Macy said that through activism and organizing she learned that

> *the kind of apathy and closed-down denial, our difficulty in looking at what we're doing to our world stems not from callous indifference or ignorance so much as it stems from fear of pain. . . . We are called to not run from the discomfort and not run from the grief or the feelings of outrage or even fear and that, if we can be fearless, to be with our pain, it turns. It doesn't stay static. It only doesn't change if we refuse to look at it.*

To avoid this grief, many people remain under the bedclothes. They trade the forest for pine-scented candles. It is uncomfortable to be awake in a sleeping world. But something has woken us from our slumber. And we have work to do. We do this work for the sleeping, but we also know that this work is in many ways in opposition to them, designed to shake them from their somnambulism, to burst the thin skins of their spheres of comfort.

They must be woken gently. We must speak to them in their language, meet them where they are and encourage them to slowly peel back the comforters to expose their eyes, their mouths, their necks and shoulders and arms and hands.

Now when they do, it is likely they will feel cold and tired and more afraid. If this is the case, we should redouble our efforts, and by that I mean: move more slowly, with more kindness, hold them closer.

Or it is possible they may feel the opposite—suddenly wide awake, sweating beneath the covers, they may feel the urge to leap to standing with zeal. This too carries risk, and we must caution them to keep seeking the truth they contain, not to ignore the brokenness they have woken to recognize within themselves. It is likely that each of us has been guilty of this ourselves. Once we've woken to it, outrage over the world can be much easier to sit with than looking at our own brokenness, and how it is affecting the people around us.

Outrage can be a different set of bedclothes, another place to hide from oneself. Surviving the work of changing the world requires that we face ourselves, that we tend to our own cracks and fissures before the pressure of the work causes us to shatter.

In 1942, Muriel Rukeyser wrote:

In time of crisis, we summon up our strength. Then, if we are lucky, we are able to call every resource, every forgotten image that can leap to our quickening, every memory that can make us know our power. And this luck is more than it seems to be: it depends on the long preparation of the self to be used.

Everything we did before we began our work prepared us for it, and everything we will become will build on who we are today. We have strength, though it's not the same strength as that of the things that terrify us. Each of us has our own particular talents and those are what we must use to continue make change in the world. Aristotle: *Where the needs of the world and your talents cross, there lies your vocation.*

Uruguayan writer Eduardo Galeano states, *Utopia is on the horizon. When I walk two steps, it takes two steps back. I walk ten steps and it is ten steps further away. What is Utopia for? It is for this, for walking.* As we walk, as we work, as we solve, the needs of the world will change. As we respond to the particulars of the terrain, become more ourselves, the talents we have will also change. This is the terror and beauty of life: discovering what it is we contain. This constant unfolding, the love of learning, our expanding love for this imperfect world and our imperfect selves.

I tell my sons: *pick a corner of the world and make it better—just take one corner and work on that. That will be enough. I tell them that, but sometimes when I look at the size of the world and the scope of its problems, problems I'm not working on, I feel like my corner is too small.*

In my wakefulness I am porous. I learn about the world and the myriad ways it is broken and feel overwhelmed. Many evenings, I grieve. I think about the rivers filled with industrial run-off, prisoners being mistreated across this country and across the world, refugees suffering, the wars erupting, the brokenness of our education system, racial inequality, workers being exploited, the pervasive loneliness of urban living, the poisoning of our bodies and minds in the interest of convenience. I think about these things and I feel as though my work is so small it will make no difference.

But then I remember that there are good people solving problems I cannot solve, reading books I haven't read. There are people stretching across the world in all directions making powerful change, more than I can mention by name—I imagine you, reader, are one of them. If each of us wakes the sleeping, there will be far more of us than there are of them. This is our work. Whichever corner of the earth we focus our attention upon.

A version of this essay was delivered as the Spring 2016 Goddard Graduate Institute Commencement Address.

ACKNOWLEDGMENTS

Some of the poems collected here were first published in slightly different versions. Many thanks to the editors of the publications who gave these words their first homes.

"Belemnite *(I dream you are in my bed)*" and "A letter to my coffin" originally appeared in *Hematopoiesis*

"Help" originally appeared in *Rogue Agent*

"I can't sleep" and "Amma, what do women want?" originally appeared in *Anomaly*

"Permission" originally appeared in *The California Journal of Poetics*

"Quartering" originally appeared in *Bellevue Literary Review*, and was later republished in Split This Rock's *The Quarry*

"This poem is want—" originally appeared in *The Offing*

"Notes on Waking the Sleeping" originally appeared in *The Feminist Wire*

In Gratitude

Honest conversation is my most essential text. I cannot hope to list all the people whose voices and ideas and reading recommendations have contributed to my thinking, but there are some names I must mention.

The poems collected here could not have been composed without the generous exchange of ideas with people I admire, particularly: Amelia Bane, Rania & Colin Campbell-Bussiere (and their extensive library), Cynthia Dewi Oka, Jimmy Santiago Baca, Colin McKee, Christiana Musk, Susanna Sonnenberg, KT Kirincic-Benevento, S.J., Sonja Swift, Eli Wright, Kevin Basl, Brendan Constantine, Mahogany L. Browne, Joy Jacobson, and Wytold Lebing (and, and and).

Most of all, my questions have been illuminated by the unextinguished light of Joe Merritt, who sets the bar for fearless self-examination. His generosity in both telling and listening and his ability to share laughter in the face of darkness have been a salve. How would I have navigated these years without you?

"Fortune" would not be without Susanna Sonnenberg

"Dear Khadija" would not be without Jimmy Santiago Baca

"Reckoning with Impermanence" would not be without Danez Smith

"Belemnite *(I dream you are in my bed)*" would not be without Jennifer Patterson

"Construction" would not be without Mahogany L. Browne

"Joy" would not be without Anne Barlieb

"Quartering" would not be without Eli Wright & Kevin Basl

A huge debt of gratitude is owed to the teachers (formal and informal) and organizations who have made space for me to grow and study as an artist despite the demands of my ordinary life: VONA, Split This Rock, Goddard College, Kundiman, and the Fine Art Work Center in Provincetown, MA.

And here, in my daily life as a working single mother in suburban Maryland, the people who have picked up the slack (or my kids) so that I could write on the edges: John Fuller, Amanda Kelly, Inshira Din, Mona Reza, Jessica Shipman, and Hooma Reza.

Thank you to the Write Bloody Publishing family for the attentive eyes, thoughtful questions, and the incredible opportunity to join the company of poets I admire so deeply.

To the veterans and service members in my writing community who have folded me into their lives and taught me what no news outlet or history book would with their willingness to voice flesh-witness accounts of the world. Thank you for refusing silence.

This book was completed with the help of a generous grant from the Arts & Humanities Council of Montgomery County.

About the Author

SEEMA REZA is the author of *A Constellation of Half-Lives* (Write Bloody Publishing, 2019) and *When the World Breaks Open* (Red Hen Press, 2016). Based outside of Washington, DC, she is the Chair & Executive Director of Community Building Art Works. She coordinates a unique multi-hospital arts program that encourages the use of the arts as a tool for narration, self-care and socialization among a population struggling with emotional and physical injuries. Her writing has appeared in print and online in *Entropy*, *The Feminist Wire*, *Bellevue Literary Review*, *The Offing*, *Full Grown People*, and *The Nervous Breakdown* among others, and has twice been nominated for a Pushcart Prize. She has performed across the country at universities, theaters, festivals, bookstores, conferences, and one fine mattress shop.

www.seemareza.com

IF YOU LIKE SEEMA REZA, SEEMA LIKES...

Birthday Girl with Possum
Brendan Constantine

Racing Hummingbirds
Jeanann Verlee

Drunks and Other Poems of Recovery
Jack McCarthy

Floating, Brilliant, Gone
Franny Choi

Counting Descent
Clint Smith

Write Bloody Publishing publishes and promotes great books of poetry every year. We believe that poetry can change the world for the better. We are an independent press dedicated to quality literature and book design, with an office in Los Angeles, California.

We are grassroots, DIY, bootstrap believers. Pull up a good book and join the family. Support independent authors, artists, and presses.

Want to know more about Write Bloody books, authors, and events? Join our mailing list at

www.writebloody.com

Write Bloody Books

CPSIA information can be obtained
at www.ICGtesting.com
Printed in the USA
FSHW012012020319